This book belongs to

_____

MY VERY FIRST
BOOK ON

GOD

The Bible version used in this publication is *The New King James Version.* Copyright © 1979, 1980, 1982, Thomas Nelson, Inc.

My Very First Book on God
ISBN 1-56292-686-1

Text copyright © 1994, 2001 by Mary Hollingsworth

Copyright © 1994, 2001 by Educational Publishing Concepts, Inc.
P.O. Box 665
Wheaton, Illinois 60189

Published by Honor Kidz
An Imprint of Honor Books, Inc.
P.O. Box 55388
Tulsa, Oklahoma 74155

MY VERY FIRST
BOOK ON

GOD

Mary Hollingsworth

Illustrated by
Rick Incrocci

HONOR
kidz

An Imprint of Honor Books, Inc.
Tulsa, Oklahoma

Dear Parents,

What is your child's concept of God? Is God a big scary ghost, who hovers overhead just waiting for us to do something wrong so He can zap us? Is God like Superman, who flies and is really strong? Or perhaps God is like Santa Claus, who operates a giant toy shop in the sky and gives us anything we want.

Well, as you know, these concepts of God are all wrong, but it's easy to understand why children come up with these ideas. These misconceptions, however, are not how you want your child to think about God.

Your child will love this book about God. It tells the child what God does, what God likes, and what God wants us to do as

His children. This is a happy book that describes our loving God. Your child will learn to love Him.

He is the God of the universe, but He is also the God of one single daisy. He is the God of unlimited power and strength, but He is also the God who wipes away a small child's tears.

Come inside and share the love and joy of God with your child—and find a bit of His love and joy for yourself, as well!

Mary Hollingsworth

There is only
one real God.
The Bible
is God's Word.

To Think About

The Bible is God's Word. Do you
love the Bible?

[There is one] God and Father of all.

Ephesians 4:6

God made the whole world.

To Do

Name some things in the world that God made.

With your crayons and paper draw a picture of God's world.

In the beginning God created the
heavens and the earth.

Genesis 1:1

God made the golden sun and the blue sky.

To Think About

What color is God's sun?
What color is God's sky?
Can you see the sun in the sky right now?

God made . . . the greater light to rule the day.

Genesis 1:16

God made the silvery moon and twinkling stars.

To Do

When it is night, ask an adult to take you outside to show you the moon and stars.

Ask an adult to help you cut a moon and some stars out of paper. Hang them in your bedroom.

God made . . . the lesser light to rule the night. [God] made the stars also.

Genesis 1:16

God made all the pretty flowers and trees.

To Do

Ask an adult to help you pick a bouquet of flowers for someone you love.

To Think About

What is your favorite kind of flower?

God said, "Let the earth bring forth grass . . . and the fruit tree."

Genesis 1:11

God made creatures that play in the water.

To Think About

Are the fish and the octopus having fun in the water?

Can you swim?

God said, "Let the waters abound with
. . . living creatures."

Genesis 1:20

God made feathered, flying birds.

To Think About

What colors do you see on these birds?

Where do God's birds usually make their houses?

God said, "Let birds fly above the earth."

Genesis 1:20

God made all the wonderful animals.

To Do

Can you name the animals in this picture?

To Think About

If you could be one of God's animals, which one would you like to be? Why?

God made the beast of the earth.

Genesis 1:25

God made people. God made me!

To Think About

Do you think that God loves people? Why?

Does God love you?

Do you love God?

Male and female [God] created them.

Genesis 1:27

God takes care of His people. God will take care of me.

To Do

Name two ways God takes care of you.

To Think About

What can you do to help take care of someone else?

Cast all your care upon Him, for He cares for you.

1 Peter 5:7

God knows all
about me.

To Do

Try to count the hairs on someone else's head.

To Think About

How do you know that God is smart?

The very hairs of your head are all numbered.

Matthew 10:30

God helps me know what to do.

To Do

What are two ways you can know what God wants you to do?

Ask an adult to help you talk to God and to read the Bible.

In all your ways acknowledge Him, and
He shall direct your paths.

Proverbs 3:6

God sends His angels to help me.

To Do

Ask an adult to read you a Bible story about an angel.

To Think About

Do God's angels protect you?

God shall give His angels charge over you.

Psalm 91:11

God always keeps His promises.

To Think About

What colors do you see in God's rainbow?

The rainbow means God keeps His promises. Do you always keep your promises?

The rainbow shall be seen . . . I will remember my [promise] . . . the waters shall never again destroy [the world].

Genesis 9:14-15

God is kind and loving.

To Think About

What are these two children doing?

To Do

Give someone you love a great big hug.

Be kind to one another.

Ephesians 4:32

God sends gentle rains to water the flowers.

To Think About

What color are the flowers in this picture?

How can you help God water the flowers?

I will give you rain in its season.

Leviticus 26:4

God wants me to talk to Him.

To Think About

Talking to God is called prayer. Have you ever talked to God before?

To Do

Ask an adult or friend to listen while you talk to God right now.

[God] hears the prayer of the righteous.

Proverbs 15:29

God loves older people.

To Do

Point to the older person in this picture.

To Think About

How is the boy showing the man that he loves him?

What older person do you love?

Do not [correct] an older man, but
[encourage] him as a father . . . older
women as mothers.

1 Timothy 5:1-2

God wants me to learn about His Word, the Bible.

To Think About

What is the girl in this picture doing?

Do you have a Bible of your very own?

To Do

Ask an adult to help you read a story from your Bible.

I will delight . . . in Your statutes; I will
not forget Your Word.

Psalm 119:16

God gives me good food to eat.

To Think About

What is your favorite kind of food?

Do you share your food with other people?

You [God] give them their food.

Psalm 145:15

God protects me while I sleep.

To Think About
Do you have happy dreams when you sleep?

To Do
Tell someone about a dream you have had.

I will both lie down in peace, and sleep;
For You alone, O LORD, make me dwell
in safety.

Psalm 4:8

God knows the name of every star in the sky.

To Do

Point to each star in this picture and give it a name.

Ask for a piece of paper and a crayon to draw your very own star. Then give it a name.

[God] counts the number of the stars;
[God] counts them all by name.

Psalm 147:4

God likes to hear me sing happy songs.

To Think About

Do you like to sing happy songs?

To Do

Sing a happy song right now.

I will sing praise to Your name, O Most High.

Psalm 9:2

God is always with me. I am never alone.

To Do

What is the child in this picture doing?

Say a prayer to thank God for watching over you.

I am with you always.

Matthew 28:20

God loves all people of all colors and all countries.

To Do

Point to each child in this picture and say, "God loves you, and I love you, too."

How many different countries can you name?

All nations shall call Him blessed.

Psalm 72:17

God wants me to tell other people about Him.

To Think About

Who would you like to tell about God?

Where are these two children going?

Go therefore and make disciples of all the nations.

Matthew 28:19

God likes to hear me laugh.

To Think About

What can you do to help someone else laugh?

To Do

The kids in this picture are laughing. Can you laugh with them?

Then our mouth was filled with laughter.

Psalm 126:2

God loves people who cannot see or hear.

To Think About

How can you show love to people who cannot hear?

How can you show love to people who cannot see?

Love one another as I have loved you.

John 13:34

God makes the wind blow where He wants it to go.

To Think About

What kind of things happen when God's wind blows?

To Do

Make a sound like the blowing wind.

He causes His wind to blow.

Psalm 147:18

God wants me to show love to others.

To Do

Think of someone to whom you can show love.

Think of a way you can show that person love.

We love because He first loved us.

1 John 4:19

God is awesome!

To Think About

What are two things you can praise God for?

To Do

Sing a happy song of praise to God.

Praise the LORD!

Psalm 147:1

God knows me and understands me very well.

To Think About

Does God know your name?

What else does God know about you?

O LORD, You have searched me and known me . . . and are acquainted with all my ways.

Psalm 139:1,3

When I am sad, God is sad, too.

To Think About

Why do you think this girl is sad?

What can you do to help someone who is sad?

[God] heals the brokenhearted.

Psalm 147:3

God wants me to visit and help sick people.

To Think About

What is the dark-haired boy in this picture doing?

To Do

Ask an adult to take you to visit someone who is sick. Take some flowers when you go.

Heal the sick . . . freely you have
received, freely give.

Matthew 10:8

God's house is a happy place to go.

To Think About

Do you like to go to church, which is God's house?

What do you do when you go to God's house?

I was glad when they said to me, "Let us go into the house of the LORD."

Psalm 122:1

God loves people who cannot walk.

To Think About

How does the girl in the picture get around?

She can do many things, just like you. Do you think she would enjoy playing with you?

Abide in My love.

John 15:9

God gave me my family to love and care for me.

To Do

What are the names of the people in your family?

Tell the members of your family that you love them right now and give them a big hug.

Honor your father and mother . . . that it may be well with you.

Ephesians 6:2-3

God's Word will show me which way to go in my life.

To Do

Ask God to help you always follow Him as you grow up.

To Think About

How will you know which way God wants you to go?

Your word is a lamp to my feet and a
light to my path.

Psalm 119:105

God lives in heaven. God wants me to live in heaven someday, too.

To Do

Use some paper and crayons to draw a picture of heaven.

Sing a song about heaven.

In my Father's house are many mansions
. . . I go to prepare a place for you.

John 14:2

God is love, and He loves me.
God wants me to love Him, too.

To Do

Make a big red heart with art paper. On it write, "Dear God, I love You." Then sign your name.

Put the red heart on the refrigerator so your family will remember to love God.

He who does not love does not know
God, for God is love.

1 John 4:8

Additional copies of this book
and other books in this series are available
from your local bookstore.

My Very First Book of Bible Fun Facts
My Very First Book of Bible Heroes
My Very First Book of Bible Lessons
My Very First Book of Prayers
My Very First Book of Bible Questions
My Very First Book of Bible Words
My Very First Book of God's Animals

If you have enjoyed this book, or if it has
impacted your life, we would like to hear from you.
Please contact us at:

Honor Kidz
Department E
P.O. Box 55388
Tulsa, Oklahoma 74155
Or by e-mail at info@honorbooks.com